BILLIONAIRES. GENIUSES. GODS. PHILANTHROPISTS.

BILLIONAIRES. GENIUSES. GODS. PHILANTHROPISTS.
"Where Greatness Outweighs Excuses"

Printed in The United States of American
Published by U&IVERSEE LLC
ISBN 979-8-218-29628-5

BILLIONAIRES. GENIUSES. GODS. PHILANTHROPISTS.

"Where Greatness Outweighs Excuseses."

Leslie "Success Story" Cosey

DEDICATION

TO ALL THE DREAMERS, who dare to venture beyond the realm of the known, to the seekers of truth, who relentlessly question the world around them, and to the quiet souls, who find comfort in the pages of a book:

This book is dedicated to you. It is a testament to the power of words, the magic of storytelling, and the undeniable influence of the human spirit. It is my hope that these pages inspire you, make you think, and most importantly, make you feel.

May you find in this book not just a story, but a piece of my soul, carefully woven into each line. May it serve as a reminder that in the vast expanse of the universe, our stories matter, your story matters.

And to my dear family, relatives, friends, associates whose un-wavering support (negatively and positively) and love and toler-ance have been my anchor in stormy seas, this book is a tribute to you. Your laughter, your tears, your wisdom, and your love - they have all found a home in these pages.

Special dediction and upmost gratatude to
My Grandfather and both my grandmother!

Everyone has **Vision**

(profound ability to perceive and embrace the hidden mysteries and interconnectedness of the universe. It is a divine gift that transcends the limitations of the physical senses, allowing individuals to glimpse into the depths of their souls and the fabric of existence itself.)

some go as far as the wall in a house, others outline the Universe."
‒ Mr. Story

TABLE OF CONTENT

Page 96: "If you're tired of people listening to yourcalls, increase in bills, forced upgrades, dropped calls screen cracking, freeze-ups, blanking out, minutes running low, constent low battery; connect to the cosmos we using telepathy over here."

Page 100: "People are so caught up looking off into space, that they are never truly present."

Page 102: "If your having an uneasy day, smoke some weed and laugh at everything that tickles your soul, if you don't smoke get some contact and watch a comedy." Laughter is an energy booster.

Page 104: "There are 3 types of prayers:
The concious prayer. The unconscious prayer. The subconcious."

Page 106: "Become the lighthouse so your future mate can see you."

Page 110: "Don't "FOLLOW ME" we follow God it's goin be a minute."

CHAPTER ONE

"LAUGH UNTIL IT HURTS THAT'S WHEN YOU EXPERIENCE TRUE HEALING."

In the depths of our souls, there lies a hidden wellspring of healing, a transformative elixir waiting to be unlocked. Picture yourself standing on the threshold of this sacred space, surrounded by a vibrant garden of laughter.

Laughter, like delicate petals unfurling under the morning sun, holds the power to transcend our pain and touch the essence of our being. It is a melody that dances upon the breeze, echoing through the chambers of our heart, resonating with joy and freedom.

Imagine a gathering of kindred spirits, their laughter intertwining like the intricate threads of a tapestry. With each shared moment of mirth, a gentle ripple of healing energy courses through their veins, embracing their wounds and dissolving the barriers that separate them from their authentic selves.

As you immerse yourself in this symphony of laughter, let it swell and crescendo until it reverberates through every fiber of your being. Feel the weight of your burdens, your worries, and your pains begin to crumble and dissolve, like autumn leaves carried away by a whimsical gust of wind.

Now, imagine the laughter intensifying, reaching a crescendo that resonates deep within your bones. As the mirth reverberates through your body, a radiant warmth spreads from your core, igniting a fiery spark of transformation. In this moment, the healing power of laughter consumes you, a torrent of energy sweeping away the shadows and embracing your spirit with pure, unadulterated light.

Laugh until it hurts, for it is within the depths of that delightful ache where the alchemy of true healing transpires. The pain becomes a bridge, connecting you to the profound wisdom of your own resilience and strength. Like a phoenix rising from the ashes, your spirit emerges renewed, unburdened, and ready to soar to new heights.

In the divine tapestry of life, laughter is the thread that stitches together our joys and sorrows, creating a vibrant mosaic of shared human experience. So, let your laughter be an offering, a sacred invocation of healing. Embrace it, cherish it, and allow it to be a balm that mends the wounds of your past and infuses your present with unbridled happiness.

May the echoes of your laughter ripple through the universe, reminding others of the transformative power that lies within. Laugh until it hurts, and in doing so, you will unveil the boundless capacity of your spirit to heal, to grow, and to embrace the beauty of this wondrous journey we call life.

"In the grand comedy of life, laughter is the standing ovation that echoes beyond the final act, reminding us that even in the face of tragedy, we hold the power to script moments of pure, unbridled joy."

ABOUT THE CREATOR

Once upon a time, in a mystical land where the celestial energies danced harmoniously with human existence, there lived a man named Mr. Success Story. His life was a tapestry woven with threads of determination, resilience, and an unwavering belief in the power of the cosmos. Mr. Success Story embraced his dual astrological heritage, guided by the nurturing essence of Cancer in American astrology and the majestic spirit of the Dragon in Chinese astrology.

In the realm of Cancer, Mr. Success Story's heartbeat with the rhythm of the ocean tides. He possessed a profound sensitivity and an intuitive connection to the emotions of those around him. The world often felt like a vast ocean, and Mr. Success Story sought to navigate its waves, bringing healing and compassion wherever he went.

One day, as Mr. Success Story walked along a moonlit beach, he encountered an ethereal figure shimmering in the darkness. It was a wise old turtle, symbolizing the ancient wisdom of the Dragon from Chinese astrology. The turtle's eyes sparkled with the secrets of the universe, and its voice resonated with the echoes of countless generations.

"Ah, Mr. Success Story," the turtle spoke with a voice that seemed to carry the weight of centuries. "Your path is illuminated by the cosmic dance of both Cancer and Dragon. In Cancer, you find the power of empathy and emotional intelligence, while in the Dragon, you embody strength, majesty, and good fortune. Embrace both, and you shall weave a destiny that transcends the ordinary."

Enlightened by the turtle's words, Mr. Success Story ventured forth, embracing the duality of his astrological heritage. With each step, he radiated the nurturing energy of Cancer, reaching out to others with love and kindness. He listened, truly listened, to the joys and sorrows of those he encountered, providing solace and guidance.

Yet, Mr. Success Story also embraced the Dragon within him. He tapped into the fire that burned within his core, a flame that fueled his ambition and drive. The Dragon's energy surged through his veins, propelling him with confidence and resilience. He fearlessly pursued his dreams, conquering challenges and soaring to new heights.

As Mr. Success Story's journey unfolded, he became a beacon of inspiration. People marveled at his ability to simultaneously embody the nurturing essence of Cancer and the majestic spirit of the Dragon. He was a living testament to the harmony he found in embracing both the gentle waves of empathy and the roaring fires of ambition.

Years passed, and Mr. Success Story's influence grew, touching countless lives. He was known not only for his accomplishments but also for his unwavering compassion and ability to empower others. His story became a testament to the limitless potential within each person, urging them to embrace their unique blend of astrological energies.

And so, Mr. Success Story continued to dance through life, a vessel of cosmic harmony. He taught the world that within the delicate balance of Cancer and Dragon, one could find the true essence of success. This success transcended material achievements and touched the depths of the soul, leaving a lasting legacy of love and inspiration.

NOTE FROM THE CREATOR

Greetings,

I pen this letter with immense joy and gratitude, for it is through the grace of the Divine that I have the opportunity to create a book that is a testament to the purity and innocence of childhood. Although intended for children, I assure you that its essence transcends age and resonates with the inner child that dwells within us all.

As the pages of this masterpiece unfolded, I listened intently to the instructions whispered by my heart, guided by a force greater than myself. Through divine connection, the book came into existence, woven with metaphors and imagery that dance across the mind like vibrant brushstrokes on a canvas. Each word and sentence will stir the depths of your imagination and touch the core of your being.

This book is not solely mine; it is ours, a shared experience that intertwines our spirits in a tapestry of wonder and discovery. It invites you to embark on a journey where the boundaries of reality blur, and the magic of the unseen becomes palpable. Together, we will traverse enchanted forests, ride unicorns through starlit skies, and befriend characters who embody our hopes, dreams, and aspirations.

Within its pages, you will notice a spiritual influence gently intertwined, guiding you toward a deeper understanding of yourself and the world around you. It whispers of the interconnectedness of all things, reminding us of the profound beauty within the simplest of moments. It encourages you to embrace your true nature and dance with the divine spark within your soul.

In closing, I invite you to open the cover of this book and embark on a journey that transcends time and space. Allow the words to ignite the fires of your imagination, to awaken the slumbering child within you. Embrace the metaphors, imagery, spiritual influence, and laughter within these pages, for they are the threads that weave together a tapestry of enchantment.

May this book be a beacon of light in your life, illuminating the path to self-discovery and reminding you of the infinite possibilities within your heart?

With love and boundless gratitude,

Leslie "Success Story" Casey

"So, my friend, rise above the doubts, embrace the challenges, and let the world witness the unstoppable force that resides within you."

"EVERYONE HAS VISION SOME GO AS FAR AS THE WALLS IN A HOUSE, OTHERS OUTLINE THE UNIVERSEE."

"Everyone has vision, some go as far as the walls in the house, others outline the universe" can be interpreted to convey the varying degrees of awareness and consciousness that individuals possess. It suggests that every person possesses the capacity for vision or perception, but the extent to which they explore and expand their understanding differs.

The phrase "some go as far as the walls in the house" implies that some individuals limit their vision to the immediate and familiar aspects of their lives. They may be unwilling or unable to venture beyond the confines of their comfort zones, restricting their awareness to what is familiar and easily comprehensible. This limited vision may be driven by fear, conditioning, or a lack of curiosity.

On the other hand, "others outline the universe" signifies individuals who possess a broader, more expansive perception. These individuals have cultivated a deeper understanding of themselves and the world around them. They have transcended the limitations of their immediate surroundings and expanded their consciousness to encompass the vastness of the universe.

They explore the mysteries of existence, seek higher truths, and strive for spiritual growth and enlightenment.

The quote, therefore, encourages individuals to reflect on the extent of their vision and awareness. It prompts them to question whether they are content with confining their perception to the walls of their own lives or if they aspire to explore the infinite possibilities and interconnectedness of the universe. It invites individuals to embark on a spiritual journey of self-discovery, expansion, and connection with the greater cosmos.

Ultimately, the quote serves as a reminder that each person has the potential to broaden their vision and explore the deeper dimensions of existence. It encourages individuals to transcend their limitations, embrace curiosity, and embark on a spiritual quest to uncover the profound mysteries of life.

Also, message is about perception, potential, and the unlimited nature of human consciousness.

"Everyone has vision" - Each person has the ability to perceive, understand, and interpret the world in their own unique way. In a spiritual sense, "vision" could refer to not only physical sight but also insight, intuition, or even spiritual revelation. It denotes that everyone has a personal perspective and a unique way of seeing and understanding the world around them.

"Some go as far as the walls in the house" - represent those who limit their understanding or perception to their immediate surroundings or physical reality. The "walls in the house" can be seen as symbolic of self-imposed limitations or boundaries, a constrained view of reality. Spiritually, it suggests a focus on the material world, the seen and known, without much exploration or consideration of the deeper, unseen, or spiritual aspects of existence.

"Others outline the universe" - This segment of the quote speaks to those

who extend their vision beyond the immediate, beyond the tangible, and into the vastness of the universe. Spiritually, it represents an expansive consciousness, a boundless perspective that seeks to understand more than what is immediately perceivable. It could refer to those who seek deeper, spiritual, or metaphysical truths, and who understand that they are part of a much larger, interconnected universe. They are not limited by the physical walls of their earthly "house," but see themselves as part of the infinite expanse of the cosmos.

The quote suggests that everyone has a certain level of vision or imagination, but the extent to which they can see or imagine varies greatly. Some people may have limited vision and only see what is immediately in front of them, represented by the walls in a house. Others, however, are able to envision and explore the vastness of the universe, represented by the wordplay of "U&IVERSEE." The quote implies that it is important to cultivate and expand one's vision in order to reach greater heights and achieve more ambitious goals.

The quote, therefore, speaks to the vast spectrum of human perception and potential. It encourages us to move beyond our self-imposed limitations and to seek a deeper, more expansive understanding of our existence. It emphasizes the spiritual belief that we are all, in essence, cosmic beings with the potential to perceive and understand the universe in its entirety.

Vision, from a spiritual perspective, can be perceived as the profound ability to perceive and embrace the hidden mysteries and interconnectedness of the universe. It is a divine gift that transcends the limitations of the physical senses, allowing individuals to glimpse into the depths of their souls and the fabric of existence itself.

For a child, vision may manifest as the innocent wonder and curiosity that sparks their imagination, enabling them to see beyond the mundane and envision limitless possibilities. It is the ability to perceive the beauty in nature, to sense the unseen energies that permeate every living being, and to dream with unbounded optimism.

As a teenager, vision becomes a transformative force, guiding them on a quest of self-discovery and purpose. It grants them the clarity to discern their authentic selves amidst societal pressures, to envision a world filled with compassion and justice, and to perceive the interconnectedness of all beings, fostering empathy and understanding.

For an adult, vision evolves into a profound spiritual insight, acquired through years of introspection and experience. It is the ability to see beyond the illusions of materialism and recognize the eternal nature of the soul. This vision enables adults to awaken their dormant potentials, align their actions with their deepest values, and serve as beacons of light for others, illuminating paths of wisdom, healing, and transformation.
Ultimately, vision, in its spiritual essence, empowers individuals of all
ages to transcend the limitations of the physical realm, align with their higher selves, and contribute to the harmonious unfolding of the universe. It is a sacred gift that invites us to explore the realms of consciousness, connect with the divine, and manifest our truest and most compassionate nature in the world.

This quote suggests that everyone has a certain level of vision or imagination, but the extent to which they can see or imagine varies greatly. Some people may have limited vision and only see what is immediately in front of them, represented by the walls in a house. Others, however, are able to envision and explore the vastness of the universe, represented by the wordplay of "U&IVERSEE." The quote implies that it is important to cultivate and expand one's vision in order to reach greater heights and achieve more ambitious goals.

SO, MY FRIEND, RISE ABOVE THE DOUBTS, EMBRACE THE CHALLENGES, AND LET THE WORLD WITNESS THE UNSTOPPABLE FORCE THAT RESIDES WITHIN YOU.

VISION

Give yourself permission
Write a vision, make it visible.
Use all available spaces

3 TYPES OF WRITERS: THE BLOCK WRITER. THE UNSURE WRITER. AND THE FREEDOM WRITER.

In the distant realms of the mind where the words reside, there lived three distinctive writers - The Block Writer, The Unsure Writer, and The Freedom Writer. Each of them was the embodiment of a different phase of the writing process that every writer experiences.

The Block Writer was an enigma, a vast desert of pure potential, cloaked in a veil of silence. His landscape was a barren plain where words seldom bloomed. He was a colossal mountain, immovable and silent, yet filled with hidden treasures. Writers would often visit him, desperate to decipher his stillness, hoping to unearth the secrets buried beneath his stony exterior.

The Unsure Writer was a restless sea, her thoughts churning and swirling like frothy waves under a stormy sky. She was a meandering river, winding aimlessly, unsure of her course, always questioning whether the words she gave birth to were worthy of seeing the light of day. She was filled with the beauty of a thousand unseen sunsets, yet she hid her brilliance behind a veil of uncertainty.

The Freedom Writer, on the other hand, was like the boundless sky. She was a radiant sun, her words poured forth like golden rays, touching everything with warmth and truth. She was a swift wind, her thoughts flowing with a sense of purpose, giving life to words as naturally as the wind gives flight to the birds. Her writing was a dance, a song, a celebration of life and its myriad experiences.

One day, in the twilight of the subconscious, they met at the crossroads of Metaphor and Imagery. The Block Writer, with his silent strength, the Unsure Writer with her turbulent thoughts, and the Freedom Writer with her radiant expression.

The Block Writer spoke first, his voice echoing like a rumble from the deepest crevice, "I am filled with ideas, yet I am silent. I yearn to express, yet words elude me."

The Unsure Writer responded, her voice like the rustling of autumn leaves, "I am filled with words, yet I am lost. I yearn to create, yet doubt clouds my path."

Finally, the Freedom Writer, her voice as clear as a mountain brook, said, "I am neither silent nor lost. I write as the bird sings, not because I have a message, but because I have a song."

Moved by her words, the Block Writer and the Unsure Writer asked, "How do you find this freedom?"

She smiled, her eyes twinkling like stars, "I let go. I let go of the fear of silence and the fear of judgment. I write not to be seen but to see, not to be heard but to hear. I write to discover, to explore, to understand. And in this journey of discovery, I find freedom."

Her words echoed in the mindscape, resonating with the silent strength of the Block Writer and the turbulent beauty of the Unsure Writer. They realized that the key to their transformation lay in embracing their true nature, accepting their fears, and writing not out of compulsion but out of love for the craft.

And so, the Block Writer began to chip away at his mountainous exterior, unearthing the hidden treasures of his thoughts. The Unsure Writer began to embrace her swirling emotions, giving voice to her deepest fears and desires. They both began to write, not as a task, but as an act of self-expression, each word a step towards self-discovery

Writer's Identification Questionnaire

Instructions: This questionnaire aims to determine your writing style and approach as either a Block Writer, Unsure Writer, or a Freedom Writer. Please answer each question honestly and to the best of your ability. Remember to trust your spiritual insight while responding. Choose the option that resonates most with your experience or preference.

1. When it comes to starting a new writing project, how do you typically feel?

a) Excited and inspired, ready to dive into the creative process.

b) Anxious or uncertain, unsure of where to begin.

c) Frustrated or blocked, struggling to find ideas or motivation.

2. How do you approach the first draft of your writing?

a) I trust my intuition and let the words flow freely without worrying about perfection.

b) I tend to overthink and edit excessively as I write, seeking perfection.

c) I often find myself getting stuck and unable to progress smoothly.

3. How do you handle writer's block or creative challenges?

a) I take breaks, engage in activities that inspire me, and connect with my inner self to find guidance and inspiration.

b) I become overwhelmed and find it challenging to overcome obstacles, often giving up easily.

c) I push through the challenges without seeking external support or alternative perspectives.

4. How do you feel about sharing your work with others?

a) I am open to receiving feedback and constructive criticism, seeing it as an opportunity to grow and improve.

b) I hesitate to share my work, fearing judgment or rejection.

c) I am defensive about my work and reluctant to make changes based on others' input.

5. How do you view the editing and revision process?

a) It is an essential part of the writing journey, embracing the opportunity to refine and polish my work.

b) I find it overwhelming and struggle to decide what needs

to be changed or improved.

c) I resist making changes or avoid revising altogether, cling-ing to the original version of my work.

6. How do you perceive the connection between spirituality and writing?

a) Writing is a spiritual practice that allows me to tap into higher wisdom and express the truth of my soul.

b) I have yet to explore the spiritual aspects of writing and see it as a purely intellectual or creative endeavor.

c) I don't consider spirituality relevant or influential in my writ-ing process.

7. How do you approach boundaries and structure in your writing?

a) I appreciate having a loose structure or outline to guide my writing while allowing room for spontaneity and creativity.

b) I feel restricted by rules or guidelines, finding it difficult to express myself authentically within predefined boundaries.

c) I need help establishing any form of structure or boundar-ies, resulting in disorganized or scattered writing.

Results:

- If you mostly answered with (a), it suggests that you resonate with the characteristics of a Freedom Writer. You have a nat-ural flow in your writing process and embrace the connection between spirituality and creativity.

- If you mostly answered with (b), it indicates that you align with the traits of an Unsure Writer. You might experience self-doubt and struggle with aspects of the writing process, poten-tially benefiting from exploring spiritual insights to find clarity.

- If you mostly answered with (c), it implies that you exhibit traits of a Block Writer.

Become the Freedom Writer

Step 1: Find Your Magical Writing Spot

Find a cozy and inspiring place where you feel comfortable and free to let your imagination soar. It could be a sunny corner of your room, a favorite park bench, or a special nook in the library.

Step 2: Gather Your Colorful Tools

Collect a set of vibrant colored pens, pencils, or markers that make you excited to write. Having a variety of colors to choose from will add a fun and creative touch to your writing.

Step 3: Create a Writing Playlist

Put together a playlist of uplifting and inspiring songs that make you happy and motivated. Play this playlist whenever you write—it will help you get into the writing groove and unleash your creativity.

Step 4: Write without Rules

Practice writing without worrying about grammar, spelling, or punctuation. Just let the words flow freely from your heart and onto the paper. Remember, there are no right or wrong answers to creative writing!

Step 5: Imagine Wildly

Close your eyes and imagine yourself in the magical world of your creation. Visualize the characters, places, and adventures you want to write about. Let your imagination run wild and see where it takes you.

Step 6: Embrace Word Play

Play with words and experiment with different writing styles. Try creating funny rhymes, tongue twisters, or even inventing your own words. The sky's the limit regarding language, so have fun and be playful with your writing.

Step 7: Write a Letter to Your Favorite Book Character

Imagine you could have a conversation with your favorite book character. Write the character in a heartfelt letter, sharing your thoughts, questions, and feelings. You might be surprised by the insights and connections that emerge.

Step 8: Take Your Writing on an Adventure

Pack a notebook and pen, and embark on a mini adventure outside. Visit a local park, beach, or even your backyard. Observe the sights, sounds, and smells around you. Let nature inspire your writing, and jot down your observations.

Step 9: Create a Storyboard

Draw or cut out pictures from magazines representing different scenes or ideas for your story. Arrange them on a large piece of paper or a bulletin board to create a visual storyboard. This will help you visualize your story and spark new ideas.

Step 10: Share Your Writing

Organize a writing circle with friends or family. Take turns reading your stories aloud and exchanging feedback and encouragement. Sharing your work with others will boost your confidence and provide valuable perspectives.

Step 11: Celebrate Your Inner Freedom Writer

Reward yourself for your writing achievements, no matter how big or small. Treat yourself to a particular writing journal, have a dance party to celebrate completing a story, or create a colorful certificate proclaiming yourself a Freedom Writer. Remember, writing is a joyful journey, so celebrate your creativity along the way!

"FAITH IS THE IDEA. LOVE IS THE ACTION.. PATIANCE IS THE OUTCOME."

In the town of Serenity, between the emerald expanse of the forest and the cerulean infinity of the sea, lived a humble sculptor named Elias. He was a man of few words, but his creations spoke volumes, interpreting his emotions into solid forms.

Faith was his stone, a marble mass of potentiality. Like the uncut slab of marble that awaited his chisel, faith was raw and real, hidden beneath layers of uncertainty. The intangible whisper beckoned Elias towards his studio every dawn, promising him that he could create something beautiful, something meaningful from the unformed stone. Faith was the morning sun that kissed the cold marble, igniting a spark of possibility in the heart of the inert stone.

Love was Elias's chisel and hammer, the tools he used to bring forth the beauty resting within the stone's heart. Each stroke was a commitment, a pledge of dedication. Love, like the chisel, shaped and molded, chipping away at the raw, unformed marble, revealing the masterpiece that lay within. It was an action, an eternal dance between the artist and his art. It was the sweat that dripped from Elias's brow, the calluses on his hands, and the tender gaze he cast upon his work.

Yet, the sculpture did not emerge in a day. It was a slow dance, a song sung in harmony with time. Patience was the melody that guided Elias's hands. It was not the lack of action, but the assurance of a rhythm, the respect for the process. It was the gentle breeze that cooled his tired body, the moonlight that kept him company through the long nights, the silent witness to his toil.

As the days turned into weeks, then months, people from far and wide would stop to watch Elias, captivated by his unwavering dedication. They saw the stone slowly transform, the formless marble metamorphosing under the sculptor's loving strokes.

And one day, the sculpture was complete. It was a breathtaking piece, a woman cradling a child, a symbol of undying love and devotion. The townspeople gathered, their faces reflecting the glow of the setting sun, their hearts filled with awe. The once unformed block of marble had been shaped into an embodiment of love, an outcome of patience.

The sculpture stood in the heart of Serenity, a silent testament to the power of faith, the act of love, and the fruit of patience. It served as a beacon of inspiration, a symbolic reminder that with faith as our foundation, love as our action, and patience as our guide, we can transform the raw, unformed stones of our life into masterpieces of beauty and meaning.

"YOU ARE GREATNESS CLOTHED IN FINE LINEN, WITH A COMPLEXION THAT MIRRORS PURE GOLD."

THE POEM

You are greatness clothed in fine linen,
With a complexion that mirrors pure gold.
In your presence, brilliance does awaken,
A story of beauty, forever to be told.

Each thread woven with grace and might,
A tapestry of dreams, resplendent and bold.
Your essence radiates with celestial light,
A testament to the treasures you hold.

In your soul, a symphony of infinite hues,
The harmony of passions, vibrant and strong.
With every step, the universe enthuses,
As you dance to the rhythm of your own song.

Your spirit, a beacon, ignites the way,
Guiding others towards their own divine quest.
Empowering hearts, bringing forth a new day,
A luminary, inspiring the very best.

Embrace the power that lies deep within,
Unleash the potential, let it unfold.
For you, dear one, carry greatness akin,

Clothed in fine linen, with a complexion of gold.
So wear your crown of magnificence high,
Embrace the journey, for it's yours to embark.
Know that you are cherished, never shy,
A masterpiece of life, a true work of art.

THE STORY

O nce upon a time, in the magical land of Lumindor, there lived a young girl named Elara. She had a heart as pure as the morning dew and a spirit as bright as the stars in the night sky. Elara lived with her grandmother, a wise and loving woman named Amara, in a cozy cottage nestled among the rolling hills.

One day, as Elara was exploring the enchanting woods near her home, she stumbled upon a shimmering golden thread that seemed to glow with its own light. Mesmerized by its beauty, she carefully picked it up and marveled at its fine texture, like the softest linen, and its complexion that mirrored pure gold.

"Grandmother, look what I found!" Elara exclaimed, rushing back to the cottage to show Amara the extraordinary thread.

Amara's eyes widened with recognition as she gently took the golden thread from Elara's hands. "My dear child, what you hold is no ordinary thread. This is the Golden Thread of Greatness, a rare and wondrous gift from the ancient weavers of destiny."

"Golden Thread of Greatness?" Elara repeated, her eyes wide with wonder.

"Yes, my dear," Amara nodded. "Legend has it that whoever possesses this thread is destined for greatness, for it holds the power to weave dreams into reality and turn the ordinary into the extraordinary."

Over time, Elara learned to cherish the Golden Thread of Greatness, treating it with the utmost care and respect. She carried it with her wherever she went, knowing that it held the key to unlocking her true potential.

As she grew older, Elara faced many challenges and obstacles, but she never lost sight of the golden thread's promise. With unwavering determination and a heart full of kindness, she used the thread to mend broken friendships, to mend broken friendships, to create marvelous works of art, and to bring hope to those in need.

One day, a great darkness threatened to engulf Lumindor, casting a shadow over the once vibrant land. Elara knew that it was her time to shine. With the Golden Thread of Greatness in hand, she embarked on a journey to confront the source of the darkness and bring light back to her beloved home.

"LOVE IS NOT MEANT TO HURT, LOVE IS MEANT TO HEAL BUT HEALING IN ITS PROCESS HURTS."

"Love is often likened to a delicate rose, a beautiful flower that possesses the power to heal the soul. Yet, within the tender petals of this bloom lies a thorny defense, a reminder that its journey to healing is not without pain. Love's thorns, they say, are the trials and tribulations that test the strength of the heart. In the garden of our existence, love is the gardener, meticulously tending to our spiritual growth. It waters the seeds of hope, cultivates the soil of compassion, and allows the sunshine of understanding to break through the clouds of ignorance.

As the gardener, love's task is not just to pluck away the weeds of despair but to prune away the dead branches of fear, shaping us into the most beautiful version of ourselves. In this process, the pruning shears may cut deep, causing us to shed tears of pain, but with each cut, a new shoot of resilience emerges. The pain of healing through love can be compared to the forging of a sword; the raw, unyielding metal subjected to intense heat and repeated blows, only to emerge as a blade of strength and purpose.

On a spiritual level, love is a divine force, an expression of the universal energy that binds all life together. It's the ever-flowing river of grace, eternally seeking to cleanse our souls of impurities. Just as a river's current may take us through turbulent rapids, love's flow can lead us through life's challenges, polishing us along the way. Love reminds us of our interconnectedness, weaving the threads of our lives into a tapestry of shared experiences.

In the grand symphony of the cosmos, love is the conductor, orchestrating harmonious melodies from the cacophony of existence. Yet, even the most beautiful symphonies require the musicians to practice and refine their skills. Love guides us through the rehearsals of life, where we stumble, make mistakes, and find our way back to the music. The process can be painful, but it's essential for the soul's growth.

In conclusion, the quote beautifully captures the paradoxical nature of love – a healer that employs pain as its chisel, a gardener that prunes with thorns, a river that washes with turbulent waters, and a conductor that turns life's cacophony into a symphony. Love, both human and divine, is the alchemical elixir that transforms suffering into growth, despair into hope, and wounds into wisdom."

"SPIRITUALLY UNIFIED, INDIVUALLY CREATED."

In a small town nestled on the outskirts of a vast forest, there lived a man named Eliah. Eliah was not just any man, however. He was known far and wide for his extraordinary talents. He could sculpt, paint, write, and even play a multitude of instruments. There was something different about Eliah, something unique and spiritual that set him apart from the rest.

Eliah's artworks were not mere trifles, but profound pieces that reflected the depths of the human soul. His sculptures were a symbiosis of nature and mankind, his paintings were a riot of emotions rendered in vibrant colors, and his writings were a mirror to his thoughts, revealing insights into the divine and the mundane.

Eliah's music, however, was his true gift. When he played, the strings resonated with the frequencies of the universe, the keys echoed the whispers of the wind, and the rhythm mirrored the heartbeat of the earth. It was as if every note he played was a spiritual connection between him, his listeners, and the cosmos.

Despite his multiplicity of talents, Eliah was not prideful. He believed that his abilities were not solely his but were a gift from the universe, a divine blessing. He saw himself as a vessel, a conduit through which the universe spoke and expressed itself. Eliah's humility was the key to his spiritual unity - despite his diverse talents, he saw them as fragments of a whole, all stemming from the same divine source.

Each day, Eliah would retreat to his humble abode by the forest. There, amid the tranquility of nature, he would meditate and tap into his spiritual essence. It was during these moments of introspection that inspiration would strike, leading to the birth of his next masterpiece.

Eliah believed that every individual was a unique creation with an innate multiplicity of talents. Through his artworks, music, and writings, he invited everyone to embark on their spiritual journey, to discover their talents, and to express their individuality.

"Spiritually Unified, Individually Created" is a celebration of Eliah's life and philosophy. It is a testament to the power of individuality and the spiritual connection that binds us all. Each image in this series captures a different facet of Eliah – the artist, the musician, the writer, and the spiritual guide – reflecting the diverse yet unified nature of his existence.

In the end, Eliah's story is not just about one man with multiple talents. It is a spiritual journey of self-discovery, a symphony of creativity, and a reminder that we are all unique, individually created beings, spiritually unified in our quest for self-expression and divine connection.

"ALLOW YOUR INNERCHILD TO BE A CHILD."

O nce upon a time, in a bustling city filled with stressed and weary adults, there lived a young woman named Maya. Maya, like many others, had forgotten the joy and wonder of her inner child as she became entangled in the complexities of adult life. Her days were consumed by deadlines, responsibilities, and the constant pursuit of success.

One evening, as Maya sat alone in her dimly lit apartment, a peculiar visitor appeared before her. It was a wise old woman who emanated an otherworldly glow. Her eyes sparkled with ancient knowledge, and her voice carried the soothing tones of a gentle breeze.

"Dear Maya," the old woman said, "I have come to remind you of the importance of allowing your inner child to be a child."

Confused yet intrigued, Maya listened intently as the wise woman continued.

"You see, dear one, your inner child is the embodiment of your purest essence. It is the part of you that dances with delight at the sound of raindrops, that marvels at the beauty of a butterfly, and that giggles uncontrollably for no apparent reason. Your inner child is the connection to the divine innocence and joy that resides within your soul."

Maya's heart stirred with a sense of longing, and she felt a distant memory awakening within her.

"As we grow older," the old woman explained, "we often suppress our inner child. We bury it beneath the weight of responsibilities, societal expectations, and the pursuit of material gains. But in doing so, we lose sight of the magic that once filled our lives."

A tear trickled down Maya's cheek as she realized the truth in the old woman's words. She yearned to rediscover the enchantment she had left behind.

The wise woman smiled warmly and extended a hand to Maya. "Come, my dear. Embrace your inner child once more. Let it soar freely, for it holds the key to your spiritual growth and fulfillment."

Maya took the old woman's hand, feeling a surge of energy course through her veins. Suddenly, the walls of her apartment dissolved, revealing a vibrant playground bathed in golden sunlight. Laughter filled the air as children frolicked and played, their spirits radiating pure joy.

Together with the wise woman, Maya joined the children in their mirthful revelry. She swung on swings, danced barefoot in the grass, and let her imagination run wild. In each moment, she felt her spirit rejuvenating, her heart expanding with love, and her connection to the divine strengthening.

Days turned into weeks, and Maya's transformation became evident to all who knew her. Her eyes sparkled with newfound wonder, and her smile reflected the radiance of her inner child. She approached her adult responsibilities with a lightness and creativity she had never experienced before.

Through the spiritual lens, Maya understood that by embracing her inner child, she had tapped into the limitless well of creativity and wisdom that resided within her soul. She had rekindled her connection to the divine source, allowing it to guide her on a path of authenticity and purpose.

And so, dear reader, let Maya's story serve as a gentle reminder for us all. In the midst of life's demands, let us not forget the importance of allowing our inner child to be a child. Nurture it, cherish it, and let it lead us back to the purest essence of our being. For it is through the innocence and wonder of our inner child that we can experience true spiritual growth and fulfillment.

As Maya continued her journey of embracing her inner child, she discovered that it was not just about engaging in childlike activities; it was a deeper spiritual practice. She began to see the world through the eyes of wonder and awe, noticing the beauty in the simplest of things—the delicate petals of a flower, the warmth of sunlight on her skin, and the melody of birdsong.

Her interactions with others transformed as well. Maya approached relationships with a childlike curiosity, free from judgment and preconceived notions. She listened attentively, without the burden of past experiences clouding her perception. Her heart overflowed with compassion, and she radiated a genuine warmth that drew others to her.

With her renewed connection to her inner child, Maya tapped into her creativity with newfound vigor. She painted, wrote stories, and danced with abandon. She allowed her imagination to roam freely, no longer bound by self-imposed limitations. In this state of playfulness, she discovered innovative solutions to problems and embarked on fulfilling projects that aligned with her true passions.

But perhaps the most profound transformation occurred within Maya's own spirit. By embracing her inner child, she reconnected with her divine essence—the part of her that was untouched by the constraints of the world. She found solace in moments of stillness, during which she communed with the sacred energy that permeated all of creation.

In these moments, Maya realized that her inner child held the key to her spiritual growth. It reminded her to live in the present moment, to surrender to the flow of life, and to trust in the divine guidance that resided within her. She understood that true wisdom came not from accumulating knowledge, but from tapping into the boundless wisdom of her inner child.

As Maya's journey continued, she inspired others to reconnect with their own inner child. She shared her story and encouraged them to embrace their innate playfulness, curiosity, and joy. The ripple effect of her transformation spread throughout the city, as more and more people rediscovered the importance of allowing their inner child to be a child.

And so, dear reader, let us heed the wisdom of Maya's story. In the midst of our adult lives, let us not forget the importance of embracing our inner child. It is through this connection that we can experience the fullness of our spiritual journey—a journey of joy, wonder, and boundless love. By allowing our inner child to be a child, we unlock the door to our own divinity and open ourselves to a world of infinite possibilities.

"BE HONEST ABOUT YOUR FEARS, THEN CONFRONT THEM."

I n a mystical realm where the boundaries of the physical and spiritual world intertwine, two friends Maya and Aiden, embark on a profound journey. They were guided by the wisdom of an ancient sage who whispered, "Be honest about your fears, then confront them."

Maya, with her long ebony hair and eyes as deep as the night sky, symbolized the depths of her inner fears. She carried the weight of her past mistakes as a heavy chain around her soul. Aiden, with his vibrant emerald eyes, with a heart as open as the fields, embodied the courage needed to confront those fears.

Their journey began in a dense forest, where shadows whispered secrets of their doubts and anxieties. The trees, gnarled and ancient, represented the tangled roots of their fears, deeply embedded in their hearts. As they walked deeper into the woods, a thick fog encircled them, blurring their path, and mirroring the confusion they often felt.

The ancient sage's voice echoed through the woods, urging them to speak their fears aloud. With trembling voices, they confessed their deepest insecurities. Maya revealed the pain of betrayal, while Aiden spoke of his fear of inadequacy.

The moment their confessions left their lips, the fog lifted, and the forest transformed into a radiant garden. Flowers of vibrant colors, representing the blossoming of their souls, began to bloom. They realized that by acknowledging their fears, they had already started to heal.

As they continued their journey, they encountered a dark and foreboding cave. The cave symbolized the ultimate confrontation of their fears. Inside, a monstrous dragon awaited them, its scales reflecting the mirror of their deepest terrors. With unwavering determination, Aiden stepped forward and extended a hand of compassion to the dragon, while Maya embraced her pain and offered it a place in her heart.

Miraculously, the dragon began to transform, its scales turning into glittering gems. As Maya and Aiden looked into the dragon's eyes, they saw their fears reflected back as mere illusions. By confronting their fears with honesty and compassion, they had tamed the dragon within.

With their newfound wisdom and inner peace, Maya and Aiden left the cave, and the world around them transformed once again. The forest was now lush and vibrant, and they were bathed in the warm light of a setting sun, signifying the end of their spiritual journey.

Hand in hand, they understood that in the realm of the heart, confronting fears and embracing them with honesty and compassion could turn darkness into radiant light, and pain into healing. The ancient sage's words had come alive, revealing the profound spiritual truth that the path to enlightenment begins with confronting one's inner dragons.

"OUR GLASSES ARE BOTH HALF EMPTY & HALF FULL."

The Dichotomy of Perception: A Glass Half Full and Half Empty. There is a profound stillness in the morning air, a quiet anticipation, like the world holding its breath before the dawn. The sun has yet to break the horizon; the day is yet to be written. And there, on the old wooden table, sits a glass - half filled with water. It stands as a parable, a metaphor for life itself, awaiting your interpretation.

Is the glass half full, or is it half empty? This simple question has been posed time and again, a philosophical quandary that seeks to understand the human disposition. The answer doesn't lie in the glass itself but in the eye of the beholder. It is a testament to our perspective, attitude, and our spiritual insight.

The half-full perspective is like the blossoming of spring after a frigid winter, a testament to optimism and hope. It's the comforting notion that every sunset is merely a precursor to a glorious sunrise. It tells a story of abundance, of appreciating the blessings we've been granted. It's the belief in the unseen good, the faith that even in the darkest clouds, there's a silver lining. It's the spiritual surrender to the idea that there's a divine plan at play, one that's always working for our greater good, even when we can't immediately see it.

This perspective nurtures gratitude, cultivates joy and fosters resilience. It's the inner light that guides us even when the external world is shrouded in darkness. It's the whispering wind telling us to dance in the rain while others seek shelter. It's the spiritual belief that every challenge we face is not a roadblock but a stepping stone towards our growth.

But what about the glass half empty? Is there worth in this seemingly pessimistic perception? In fact, might it not be pessimism, but

realism in another guise?

Doesn't the half-empty glass also have a lesson to teach? Like the moon in the night sky, it reflects the darker aspects of life, the shadows that give depth and meaning to our existence. It's the stark reminder that life is not always sunshine and summer breezes, but also storms and biting frost. It's the acceptance of the fact that pain, loss, and hardship are as much part of our journeys as joy, gain, and ease.

The half-empty perspective is a call to action, a stimulus for change. It's the understanding that we are co-creators of our destiny, that we have the power and the responsibility to fill the empty space in our glasses. It's the spiritual insight that the void we experience is an invitation to seek, to strive, to grow.

It's the acknowledgement that we are incomplete beings in pursuit of wholeness.

CHAPTERTWO

"LISTEN TO YOUR MIND, THEN FOLLOW YOUR HEART."

Listen to your mind, then walk with your heart,' carries a profound spiritual connotation. It suggests an introspective journey that everyone must undertake to lead a fulfilling and enlightened life.

'Listening to your mind' can be envisioned as standing at the edge of a vast, echoing cavern, the embodiment of our thoughts and intellect. In the heart of this cavern, whispers of logic, reason, and conscious thoughts resonate, bouncing off the stone walls. These echoes symbolize the mental processes that guide our decisions, and listening to them is akin to holding a lantern in the darkness, illuminating the path of wisdom and discernment.

However, the journey doesn't end there. 'Then walk with your heart,' brings forth the image of a radiant sun setting over a tranquil sea, painting the canvas of the sky with hues of compassion, love, and empathy. Walking with your heart is like taking off your shoes to feel the warm sand beneath your feet and immerse yourself in life's rhythm. It is to allow the tides of emotions, the waves of compassion and love, to guide your steps on the shoreline of existence.

Therefore, the spiritual essence of the quote is a harmonious dance between the mind and heart, a refined balance between intellect and emotion. It emphasizes the importance of using our cognitive abilities to understand the world but also encourages us to engage our heart's innate wisdom to experience life fully. In this dance, every step taken with the mind's clarity is followed by a move made with the heart's warmth, creating a beautiful symphony of enlightened living."

'Listening to your mind' can be envisioned as standing at the edge of a vast, echoing cavern, the embodiment of our thoughts and intellect. In the heart of this cavern, whispers of logic, reason, and conscious thoughts resonate, bouncing off the stone walls. These echoes symbolize the mental processes that guide our decisions, and listening to them

is akin to holding a lantern in the darkness, illuminating the path of wisdom and discernment.

However, the journey doesn't end there. 'Then walk with your heart,' brings forth the image of a radiant sun setting over a tranquil sea, painting the canvas of the sky with hues of compassion, love, and empathy. Walking with your heart is like taking off your shoes to feel the warm sand beneath your feet and immerse yourself in life's rhythm. It is to allow the tides of emotions, the waves of compassion and love, to guide your steps on the shoreline of existence.

Therefore, the spiritual essence of the quote is a harmonious dance between the mind and heart, a refined balance between intellect and emotion. It emphasizes the importance of using our cognitive abilities to understand the world but also encourages us to engage our heart's innate wisdom to experience life fully. In this dance, every step taken with the mind's clarity is followed by a move made with the heart's warmth, creating a beautiful symphony of enlightened living." include a master teaching people how to listen to their mind, then follow their heart and why it helps.

THE STORY OF RISHI ARJUNA, THE WISE MASTER OF " LISTEN TO YOUR MIND, THEN FOLLOW YOUR HEART."

IN a quaint village, amidst rolling hills and lush forests, there lived a wise master known as Rishi Arjuna. He was renowned throughout the land for his profound teachings and his ability to guide people on the path of self-discovery. His humble abode was perched atop a hill, overlooking a serene valley, where the whispers of the wind and the melodies of the birds were in perfect harmony. It was said that the very air around him carried the scent of enlightenment.

One crisp morning, as the sun began its ascent, a group of seekers, hungry for wisdom, gathered at the foot of the hill. They had heard tales of Rishi Arjuna's teachings and sought to unravel the secrets of leading a fulfilled and enlightened life.

Rishi Arjuna welcomed them with a warm smile and invited them to sit in a circle beneath the shade of a sprawling banyan tree. His eyes, deep and reflective, seemed to hold the wisdom of ages.

"Listen to your mind, then walk with your heart," he began, his voice like the gentle rustle of leaves in a breeze. "This is the essence of the path I shall guide you on today."

With these words, he asked the seekers to close their eyes and take a deep breath. "Imagine," he continued, "that your mind is a vast cavern, deep and echoing. Inside this cavern, the whispers of logic, reason, and conscious thoughts resound."

As the seekers embraced this imagery, they felt themselves transported to the edge of a grand cavern, surrounded by darkness. Within, they could hear the echoes of their own thoughts, like distant ripples on a tranquil pond.

"The cavern of your mind," Rishi Arjuna explained, "represents your intellect and the power of discernment. By listening to these echoes, you illuminate the path of wisdom, enabling you to make choices that align with your true self."

The seekers nodded in understanding, their minds now focused on the echoes of their inner thoughts, which seemed to grow clearer with each passing moment.

"Now," Rishi Arjuna continued, "imagine that you are descending deeper into this cavern, where the whispers of your heart await."

As they ventured further into the cavern of their minds, the seekers felt a profound shift. They found themselves surrounded by a gentle radiance, as if the very walls of the cavern were imbued with love and compassion.

"In the heart of your cavern," Rishi Arjuna elucidated, "lies your emotional intelligence, the reservoir of empathy, love, and compassion. Walking with your heart is akin to removing your shoes and feeling the warm sand beneath your feet. It is surrendering to the rhythms of life and allowing your heart's wisdom to guide your steps."

In this inner journey, the seekers felt their hearts beating in harmony with the universe, and a profound sense of interconnectedness washed over them.

"The dance between your mind and heart," Rishi Arjuna concluded, "creates the symphony of enlightened living. Your mind offers clarity and understanding, while your heart provides warmth and empathy. When

you integrate these aspects of yourself, you lead a life that is not only fulfilling but also enriching for those around you."

As the seekers opened their eyes, they realized that the hilltop, which had been a tranquil setting, now seemed imbued with a deeper beauty. The rustling leaves and the songs of birds took on new meaning, as they understood the balance between intellect and emotion, mind and heart.

With gratitude in their hearts, they bowed to Rishi Arjuna, who had illuminated their path to enlightenment. And as they descended the hill, they knew they would carry the wisdom of his teachings with them, walking with their minds and hearts in perfect harmony, creating a symphony of love and understanding in their own lives and the world around them.

"THE MIND PLAYS TWO PARTS, THE PARTICIPANT & THE DISTRACTION"

In a quaint village amidst lush green fields, there lived a young boy named Timmy. Timmy had an extraordinary gift. He could see the world in a special way that few people could understand.

Timmy believed that the mind was like a beautiful garden. He imagined that in this garden, there were two little creatures: the Distraction and the Participant. The Distraction was mischievous and loved to play tricks on the Participant. It would jump from one flower to another, making them sway in the wind and capturing the Participant's attention. The Distraction would whisper stories and worries like wind blowing through the garden.

One sunny day, as Timmy was sitting 0in the shade of a tall oak tree, he noticed the Distraction hopping from flower to flower, trying to catch the Participant's attention. The Participant, on the other hand, was a calm and peaceful creature, curious about the wonders of the garden. It loved to explore and learn new things.

Timmy realized that the Distraction was preventing the Participant from enjoying the beauty of the garden. He understood that the Distraction's tricks were like clouds covering the bright sun, making it hard for the Participant to see the true colors of life.

With determination in his eyes, Timmy decided to take action. He gently approached the Distraction and spoke softly, "Dear Distraction, I understand that you want to have fun and play, but you are stopping the Participant from experiencing the wonders of this garden. Can we find a way for both of you to coexist?" The Distraction paused for a moment, contemplating Timmy's words. It realized that by constantly playing tricks, it was missing out on the joy of exploring the garden alongside the Participant. The Distraction smiled and nodded in agreement.

From that day forward, the Distraction and the Participant became best friends. They no longer played tricks on each other, but instead, they worked hand in hand. Whenever the Distraction started to jump from flower to flower, the Participant gently reminded it to slow down and appreciate the moment. Likewise, when the Participant started to feel overwhelmed, the Distraction would bring a bit of cheerfulness to brighten their day.

Timmy learned a valuable lesson from this experience. He understood that our minds are like gardens, too. We have the power to choose how we want to experience life. If we let the Distraction take over, we may miss out on the beauty and magic surrounding us. But if we allow the Participant to guide us, we can explore the world with curiosity and gratitude.

So, my dear child, remember that you have the power to be the Participant in your own mind's garden. Embrace the wonders around you, stay focused on what brings you joy, and let the Distraction be a playful companion rather than a hindrance. In this way, you will find harmony and peace within yourself, and the vibrant colors of life will always shine brightly for you to enjoy.

STEPS TO IMPROVE

Understanding and balancing the two aspects of the mind.

1. **Awareness:** Start by becoming aware of the Distraction and the Participant within your mind. Notice when the Distraction tries to take over, causing your thoughts to wander or worry unnecessarily. Similarly, recognize the calm and curious nature of the Participant, which allows you to focus and engage fully in the present moment.

2. **Mindfulness:** Practice mindfulness to strengthen your ability to stay present and attentive. When you catch the Distraction trying to pull you away from the task, gently acknowledge its presence without judgment. Then, bring your attention back to the Participant, embracing its curiosity and eagerness to participate fully in the moment.

3. **Intention:** Set clear intentions for your actions and experiences. Before starting a task or engaging in an activity, ask yourself, "What is my purpose here? What do I hope to achieve or learn?" By setting intentions, you provide guidance to both the Distraction and the Participant, steering them towards a common goal.

4. **Prioritization:** Learn to prioritize your focus and energy. While the Distraction may offer tempting diversions, evaluate whether they align with your intentions and goals. Sometimes, it's necessary to let go of distractions that hinder your progress or well-being, allowing the Participant to take the lead in pursuing what truly matters to you.

5. **Balance and Harmony:** Understand that balance doesn't

mean eliminating the Distraction entirely. Instead, aim for a harmonious relationship between the two. Let the Distraction bring moments of lightness and playfulness into your life, but always bring it back to the Participant's grounded presence. Find a rhythm that allows the two aspects to coexist, supporting each other rather than conflicting.

6. **Self-Compassion:** Be kind to yourself throughout this journey of understanding and balance. It's natural to occasionally get carried away by the Distraction or struggle to focus with the Participant. Remember that it takes practice and patience. Treat yourself with compassion, gently guiding your mind back towards equilibrium whenever it veers off course.

By cultivating awareness, practicing mindfulness, setting intentions, prioritizing, seeking balance, and embracing self-compassion, you can develop a deeper understanding of the Distraction and the Participant within your mind. This understanding will empower you to maintain a harmonious balance, allowing you to engage fully in life's experiences while staying focused and present in the moment.

THE MIND SEES.
THE HEART BEATS.
THE BODY MOVES.

The mind sees. The heart beats. The body moves" carries profound significance that reflects the interconnectedness of various aspects of human existence.

"The mind sees" refers to the power of perception and awareness. It signifies the ability of the human mind to observe and comprehend the world around us, including both the physical and metaphysical realms. From a spiritual perspective, it implies the capacity to perceive beyond the surface level and to gain insights into the deeper truths and mysteries of life.

"The heartbeats" expresses the essence of emotions, love, and compassion. Spiritually, the heart is the seat of the soul and represents the center of our being. It symbolizes our capacity for empathy, connection, and spiritual growth. The heart's beating signifies the life force within us, the rhythm of existence, and the universal energy that flows through all living beings.

"The body moves" alludes to the physical vessel through which we interact with the world. In a spiritual context, the body is considered a vehicle for the soul's experience and evolution. It represents the instrument through which we express ourselves, take action, and manifest our intentions. The body's movements can be seen as an external manifestation of our inner state, reflecting our thoughts, emotions, and spiritual alignment.

Combined, these three statements highlight the unity of the mind, heart, and body in the spiritual journey. They emphasize the integrated nature of our existence, suggesting that spiritual growth and fulfillment occur when these aspects are in harmony. The mind's perception, the heart's love, and the body's actions synergistically contribute to our spiritual development, allowing us to navigate the world with wisdom, compassion, identity and purpose.

THE BLACK MAN'S SUPERPOWER IS HIS NUTTSACK, WITH ABSTINENCE, AND THE BLACK WOMAN HE CAN (SEE) HIS VISION..

"

Imagine a vast and magnificent garden, where each plant represents an individual's spiritual essence and potential. In this garden, the Black man's superpower can be likened to a seed—a seed that holds within it the power to create and nurture life. Just as a seed contains the blueprint for a mighty tree, the Black man's seed represents his unique potential to manifest and bring forth his visions and aspirations.

However, the seed alone is not enough to realize its full potential. It requires the nurturing influence of the Black woman, who represents the embodiment of wisdom, intuition, and nurturing energy. In this metaphorical garden, the Black woman's presence is like the sunlight, providing illumination and clarity to the Black man's vision. With her by his side, the Black man can gain a profound understanding of his purpose and tap into his full creative potential.

To further deepen our understanding, let us explore the concept of abstinence as a powerful force within this spiritual allegory. Just as a gardener selectively prunes certain branches to allow the tree to flourish, abstinence can be seen as the conscious choice to abstain from distractions and negative influences that may hinder the Black man's growth and vision. By practicing abstinence, he cultivates discipline and focus, enabling him to channel his energy and creativity into realizing his true potential.

When the Black man's seed, representing his potential, merges with the Black woman's nurturing energy and wisdom, a profound unity emerges. They become harmonious partners, each contributing their unique strengths to create a fertile ground for personal and spiritual growth. In this sacred union, the Black man can fully "see" his vision, experiencing a heightened level of clarity, purpose, and spiritual connection.

This metaphorical journey invites us to contemplate the transformative power of unity, abstinence, and the harmonious partnership between the Black man and woman. It emphasizes the potential for greatness and spiritual realization that lies within each individual, and the significance of nurturing relationships, discipline, and focus in manifesting one's vision and purpose in life.

"MONEY MAKES ALL OF US FEEL A CERTAIN WAY, THAT FEELING OF EMPOWERMENT WHEN WE HAVE IT. DO THIS, FEEL THAT SAME EMPOWERMENT WITHOUT MONEY, SHIT, WITHOUT HAVING ANYTHING, AND WATCH YOUR LIFE BEGIN TO HAPPEN. THE MORE FEEL EMPOWERED THE MORE YOU WILL ATTRACT THE THINGS YOU WANT."

From a spiritual perspective, the statement suggests that money carries a particular energy or vibration that affects our emotions and sense of personal power. When we possess money, it often brings a feeling of empowerment and security. However, the message encourages us to explore the possibility of experiencing that same sense of empowerment and abundance without relying solely on material possessions.

In this interpretation, it proposes that true empowerment and the ability to manifest the things we desire come from within ourselves, rather than from external circumstances or material wealth. It invites us to tap into our inner strength, confidence, and sense of self-worth, independent of material possessions.

By cultivating a strong internal state of empowerment, we emit a certain energy or vibration that attracts positive experiences and desired outcomes into our lives. In other words, the more we align with feelings of personal power and abundance, the more we are to attract the things we desire.

This spiritual perspective implies that our thoughts, emotions, and beliefs play a significant role in shaping our reality. By consciously choosing to feel empowered, even in the absence of material wealth, we open ourselves up to new possibilities and opportunities. It suggests that our focus should be on developing a deep sense of self-empowerment rather than relying solely on external factors such as money or possessions to define our worth or happiness.

In summary, this interpretation encourages us to recognize the inherent power within ourselves and the role our emotions and mindset play in manifesting our desires. It suggests that true empowerment and attraction of the things we want come from cultivating a strong internal state of being, regardless of our external circumstances.

"IF 10% OF YOUR TITHE (TIME) CAN MAKE A PASTOR RICH/WEALTHY. 10 % OF YOUR 24-HOUR DAY CAN GIVE A CHILD(REN) THEIR LIFE(LIVES) BACK. IT ONLY TAKES 2 HOURS AND 40 MINS."

Metaphorically speaking, a pastor's wealth or richness can be associated with the growth and prosperity of their religious congregation. By devoting 10% of their time, effort, and resources to their pastoral duties, such as preaching, counseling, and organizing community activities, the pastor may gain popularity, influence, and support from their followers. This can lead to financial benefits, such as increased donations or offerings, which contribute to their personal wealth.

On the other hand, when we consider the life of a child in a spiritual sense, the metaphorical significance of giving 10% of your 24-hour day takes on a different meaning. Here, the focus shifts towards the potential impact of investing time and attention in nurturing a child's spiritual well-being. By spending quality time, providing guidance, and cultivating an environment conducive to their growth, we "give a child their life back."

In this metaphorical sense, a child's life may refer to their spiritual vitality, emotional well-being, and overall development. By allocating a significant portion of your time (10% of a day) to this purpose, you are investing in their spiritual foundation. This investment can encompass activities such as sharing wisdom, teaching moral values, offering emotional support, and fostering a sense of identity and purpose. Through such efforts, a child's life can be metaphorically transformed, reinvigorated, and enriched.

We can visualize the contrast between the pastor's enrichment and the child's spiritual restoration. Imagine a scale where the pastor's wealth is symbolized by gold coins accumulating on one side, representing the material benefits that come with their success. Meanwhile, on the other side, we see a barren tree springing back to life, with vibrant leaves and blossoms representing the rejuvenated spiritual essence of a child.

This highlights the divergent outcomes that can arise when dedicating a fraction of one's time. While the pastor's enrichment may be associated with financial abundance, the investment of time and energy in a child's spiritual well-being brings forth a profound transformation that nourishes their inner growth and restores their vitality.

THINK ABOUT THAT

It only takes 2 hours and 40 mins a day, to invoke awareness." a small amount of daily time investment, represented as 2 hours and 40 minutes, (the length of time a service last) can be transformational. Spiritually, it suggests that individuals can cultivate a heightened awareness or consciousness by actively engaging in spiritual practices, such as meditation, prayer, self-reflection, or seeking knowledge.

IDENTITY & PURPOSE

Identity and purpose are two fundamental aspects of human life that are deeply intertwined. Our identity is who we are as individuals, shaped by a combination of factors such as our upbringing, experiences, beliefs, and values. Our purpose, on the other hand, is the reason why we exist and what we strive to accomplish in life.

For many people, their sense of identity is closely tied to their purpose. They find meaning and fulfillment in pursuing goals that align with their values and beliefs. This can take many forms, such as pursuing a career that they are passionate about, engaging in activities that bring them personal fulfillment, or contributing to causes that they believe in.

However, for others, the relationship between identity and purpose can be more complex. They may struggle to define their identity, or they may feel that their purpose is unclear or elusive. This can lead to feelings of confusion, dissatisfaction, or even despair.

One way to cultivate a deeper sense of identity and purpose is to engage in self-reflection. This can involve asking ourselves questions such as:

- What are my core values and beliefs?
- What are my strengths and weaknesses?
- What brings me joy and fulfillment?
- What impact do I want to make in the world?

By taking the time to reflect on these questions, we can gain a better understanding of who we are and what we want to achieve. We can also begin to identify the actions we can take to align our lives more closely with our values and purpose.

It's important to note that our sense of identity and purpose can evolve over time. What may have been important to us in the past may no longer hold the same significance, and new experiences and challenges may lead us to redefine our sense of self and purpose. Therefore, it's important to engage in ongoing self-reflection and be open to new opportunities and experiences that can help us grow and evolve.

In conclusion, identity and purpose are two deeply interconnected aspects of human life that play a crucial role in our sense of fulfillment and happiness. By taking the time to reflect on who we are and what we want to achieve, we can cultivate a deeper sense of meaning and purpose in our lives.

"IT'S ONLY PAIN UNTIL WE RELEARN TO EXPERIENCE IT AS POWER!.."

They say the ocean's strength lies in its depth, and just like the ocean, my pain runs deep. But it's in this depth that I find my power. As I embrace the ebb and flow of life's challenges, I emerge stronger, more resilient, and ready to conquer whatever comes my way.

Pain may be my constant companion, but I've learned to harness its energy, transforming it into a force that propels me forward. So, let the waves of life crash upon me, for I know that with each wave, I'll rise higher, rising above my circumstances with newfound strength.

Let us remember that our pain doesn't define us; rather, it shapes us into the warriors we're meant to be. Share your story, embrace your journey, and let your pain be the current that drives you to greatness.

In a small, vibrant community nestled amidst the lush greenery, a wise melanin man named Malik gathered a group of individuals under the shade of a towering oak tree. His presence radiated an aura of calmness and wisdom, drawing everyone's attention. The group consisted of people from different walks of life, each carrying their own burdens of pain and suffering.

As the golden rays of the setting sun filtered through the leaves, casting a warm glow on the faces of the listeners, Malik began to speak. His voice resonated with a deep conviction, carrying with it the weight of his own life experiences.

"Every one of you has known pain," Malik said, his eyes filled with empathy. "But what if I told you that pain is not a curse to be endured, but a seed of power waiting to be nurtured within you?"

Curiosity sparked in the eyes of those gathered, and they leaned in closer, captivated by his words. Malik continued, painting vivid images with his poetic metaphors and invoking spiritual insights.

"Pain, my friends, is like a storm that rages within us," he explained. "It lashes against our souls, threatening to tear us apart. But if we can learn to harness its energy, we can turn that storm into a force of power and transformation."

He raised his hand, pointing to the oak tree that sheltered them. "Look at this majestic tree. Its roots run deep, anchoring it to the earth. With every fierce gust of wind, the tree bends, but it does not break. It draws strength from adversity, just as we can draw strength from our pain."

The group nodded, captivated by the imagery. Malik continued, "No flower blooms without enduring the darkness of the soil. No diamond shines without enduring the pressure of the earth. Similarly, our pain is the crucible that can shape us into our truest selves."

He paused, allowing his words to sink in. "To transform pain into power, we must first acknowledge it. We must sit with our pain, embrace it, and understand its lessons. Only then can we begin the process of healing and growth."

A woman in the crowd spoke up, her voice trembling with vulnerability. "But how can we find power in our pain? How can we rise above it?"

Malik smiled, his eyes filled with compassion. "By choosing how we respond," he replied. "In the face of pain, we have a choice: to let it consume us or to rise above it. We can allow pain to define us, or we can use it as a stepping stone toward our own greatness."

He leaned forward, his voice filled with conviction. "Life's greatest lessons often emerge from our most challenging experiences. Pain is a teacher, guiding us toward our own strength, resilience, and compassion. It is through pain that we learn empathy, humility, and the power of forgiveness."

The group fell into a contemplative silence, absorbing Malik's profound wisdom. Each individual began to reflect on their own pain, seeing it with newfound clarity and purpose. They realized that within their struggles lay the seeds of their own transformation and empowerment.

As the sun dipped below the horizon, casting the world into a gentle twilight, Malik concluded his discourse. "Remember, my friends, pain is not the end of the story. It is merely a chapter in the book of your life. Embrace it, learn from it, and let it fuel the fire within you

#PainAsPower #StrengthInStruggle #RiseAboveTheTide

CHAPTER THREE

BILLIONAIRES. GENIUSES GODS PHILANTHROPISTS

1. **Melanin Billionaires:** Born of stardust and earthly roots, these children possessed skin that glistened like the night sky. Their wealth extended beyond material riches, as they amassed treasures of compassion and empathy, investing in the betterment of humanity.

2. **Melanin Geniuses:** Their minds were galaxies of knowledge, with neurons sparking like distant stars. These brilliant minds unraveled the universe's secrets, shedding light on mysteries that had long eluded human understanding.

3. **Melanin Gods:** Not deities, but embodiments of humanity's divine potential. They radiated purpose and humility, reminding us of the spiritual essence within. Their presence stirred souls and ignited a collective yearning to transcend the ordinary.

4. **Melanin Philanthropists:** With hearts as vast as the cosmos, these children turned kindness into currency. Their selflessness built bridges between worlds, showering a world often parched by greed with the nourishing rain of their generosity.Born under the watchful eye of the moon, these children were destined to be billionaires not only in wealth, but in compassion. Their hearts, as expansive as the cosmos, knew no bounds in generosity. They transformed the currency of kindness into a

wealth that transcended mere material possessions. Through their philanthropic endeavors, they built bridges between the tangible and the intangible, showering a world parched by greed with the rain of their benevolence.

As their intellect shone brighter than the sun, these melanin geniuses unraveled secrets hidden within the fabric of existence. Like master alchemists, they transformed curiosity into profound innerstanding, transmuting ignorance into enlightenment. With minds like supernovae, they cast light into the dark corners of ignorance, revealing the interconnectedness of all knowledge, weaving intricate patterns of truth and insight.

Guided by an inner compass, these children were seen as modern-day gods, not in the sense of divinity, but as embodiments of the divine potential within humanity. Their existence was a testament to the infinite possibilities hidden within each soul. They radiated an aura of purpose and humility, reminding humanity of its capacity to rise above the mundane and embrace the extraordinary.

As they walked the path of life, their footprints left imprints of hope, each step echoing with the resonance of a spiritual symphony. Like cosmic wanderers, they found solace in the beauty of both the seen and the unseen, understanding that life's true meaning lay in the harmony of contrasts.

In the end, their story was a living testament to the boundless potential of human existence, a melody of triumph composed with the notes of melanin, brilliance, compassion, and unity. Their journey was a reminder that within each soul resides the power to be a billionaire of love, a genius of understanding, a god of potential, and a philanthropist of the heart.

In the mystical realm of imagination, where dreams unfold like ethereal tapestries, there existed a generation of children unlike any other. Born with minds that ignited with the brilliance of a thousand suns, they were destined to become the architects of a new world—a world where boundaries of possibility were shattered, and profound secrets of existence were unraveled.

These children, adorned with the crowns of destiny, possessed hearts that overflowed with compassion and an insatiable thirst for knowledge. They were the billionaires of benevolence, their wealth measured not in treasures of gold, but in the depth of their understanding and the magnitude of their love for humankind.

Their minds, like celestial maps, were interconnected with cosmic threads, weaving together their collective genius. Each child, blessed with a unique gift, held a piece of the puzzle that would unlock the mysteries of the universe. One had an intuitive grasp of mathematics, while another possessed a profound understanding of the arts. One was a prodigious scientist, while another reveled in metaphysics.

Like gods of a new era, these young visionaries embarked on a sacred quest to illuminate the darkness that plagued the world. With every step, they left footprints of inspiration, igniting the dormant sparks of brilliance within the hearts of others. Their minds, like cosmic lighthouses, guided lost souls toward the shores of enlightenment.

And so, the tale of these children billionaires, geniuses, gods, and philanthropists serves as a testament to the extraordinary power within the human spirit. It reminds us that, regardless of age or circumstance, we all can shape destinies and transform the world with the light of our souls.

"LEARN THE LANGUAGE OF THE UNIVERSE THE STILL SMALL VOICE."

In a tranquil village nestled between rolling hills, there lived a young girl named Elara. She possessed a gift that set her apart from the others—a profound ability to listen not just with her ears, but with her heart. She could hear the whispers of the wind, decipher the melodies of the rustling leaves, and feel the rhythm of the earth beneath her feet. This gift was bestowed upon her by the Mystical Weaver, an enigmatic figure said to have woven the fabric of the universe with threads of wisdom and insight.

Elara's village was bustling with noise—chatter filled the air, opinions clashed, and distractions were aplenty. Amidst this chaos, the villagers struggled to hear the gentle guidance that emanated from the cosmic tapestry, the "still small voice" woven into the very fabric of existence.

But Elara was different. She spent her days wandering through the verdant meadows, sitting by the babbling brook, and climbing the ancient oak trees. She learned to attune her senses to the symphony of nature, understanding that the whispers carried messages of profound significance.

One fateful evening, as the sun dipped below the horizon and the stars began their nightly dance across the sky, Elara found herself atop a hill overlooking the village. A gentle breeze enveloped her, and she closed her eyes, allowing herself to become one with the world around her. In that moment of stillness, she heard a faint yet resounding voice—a cosmic murmur that spoke directly to her soul.

"Elara," the voice whispered, "listen with your heart, for within its chambers resides the key to unlocking the secrets of the universe. Tune your senses to the vibrations of creation, and you shall find guidance in every whisper, every rustle, and every beat."

With these words etched into her being, Elara returned to her village, her spirit illuminated by newfound clarity. She shared her wisdom with those willing to listen, teaching them to quiet the cacophony of daily life and embrace the symphony of the cosmos.

As time passed, Elara's village transformed. The once tumultuous air became filled with tranquility and understanding. The villagers learned to listen—to truly hear—the "still small voice" that resonated within and around them. They discovered that the divine spoke not in thunderous roars but in the gentlest of whispers, guiding them towards holistic and divine direction.

In learning to listen, Elara and her village found themselves in harmony with the rhythms of the universe. They understood that within the silence lay the most profound revelations, and by tuning in, they received the guidance of the Most High in the whispers of the wind, the rustle of leaves, and the beating of their own hearts.

INTUITION AND INSTINCTS

The concepts of intuition and instincts, often associated with feminine and masculine qualities respectively, can be understood metaphorically in a spiritual context.

Intuition (Feminine):
Intuition is like a deep, flowing river within us, symbolizing receptivity, inner wisdom, and emotional intelligence. It's often associated with the feminine because it emphasizes empathy, nurturing, and the ability to connect with the subtle energies of the universe. Intuition is like a compass guiding us through the unseen currents of life, helping us understand the emotions and needs of ourselves and others.

Benefits of Knowing Intuition (Feminine):
When we tap into our intuition, we gain access to our inner guidance system. This can help us make empathetic and compassionate decisions, fostering harmonious relationships and a deep understanding of the world around us. Intuition enables us to navigate life's challenges with grace and emotional intelligence.

Instincts (Masculine):
Instincts are akin to a sturdy tree firmly rooted in the ground, symbolizing strength, protection, and survival. They are often associated with the masculine because they represent assertiveness, action, and the ability to respond swiftly to external stimuli. Instincts are like a shield, guarding us against threats and enabling us to take decisive action.

Benefits of Knowing Instincts (Masculine):
When we harness our instincts, we become more resilient and capable of protecting ourselves and our loved ones. This can lead to a sense of security and empowerment. Instincts help us face challenges head-on and navigate the physical world effectively.

Connection and Benefits of Balancing Both:
In a holistic spiritual understanding, the synergy between intuition and instincts is crucial. Like the yin and yang, they complement each other. Integrating both aspects allows us to achieve balance and harmony.

Knowing one's intuition can help us tune into the deeper layers of our consciousness, guiding our actions with empathy and understanding. Meanwhile, knowing our instincts provides us with the strength and courage to act upon our intuitive insights. Together, they empower us to make decisions that are not only emotionally intelligent but also practical and protective.

In essence, recognizing and embracing both intuition and instincts allows us to become more whole and spiritually aligned beings, capable of navigating the complexities of life with grace and wisdom.

Once upon a time, in the heart of a bustling city, there lived two remarkable individuals - a woman named Intuition, and a man named Instincts. Born on the same day, month, and year (June 29, 1976), their bond was as unique as their names. They shared a friendship that was deep and enduring, built on mutual respect and understanding.

Intuition, a meditation instructor and healer was known for her gentle demeanor and profound wisdom. She had a knack for sensing what lay beneath the surface, guiding her students through their emotional landscapes with remarkable insight and patience. Her classes were sought after, with people claiming that her teachings had a transformative impact on their lives.

On the other hand, Instincts was a renowned photographer and marketing genius. His evocative work moved hearts, and his marketing strategies revolutionized businesses. He had an uncanny ability to capture the essence of any moment - a skill that extended beyond his photography and into his philanthropic endeavors. He inspired people not just through his work, but also through his actions, using his considerable influence to champion causes that needed attention.

Although their professions were vastly different, Intuition and Instincts were intrinsically connected, each complementing the other. Instincts' boldness and action-oriented nature offset Intuition's calm, introspective personality. They often consulted each other, with Intuition providing Instincts with deep insights into human behavior and Instincts offering Intuition innovative ways to reach more people with her teachings.

One day, Instincts approached Intuition with an idea. He wanted to create a campaign that would inspire people to take action for a cause dear to him - improving mental health awareness. Instincts had the marketing expertise and the resources, but he needed Intuition's knowledge and experience to ensure that the campaign resonated on a deeper level.

Intuition was enthusiastic about the idea. She knew the profound impact that mental health had on overall well-being and was eager to contribute to a cause that could help many.

She provided Instincts with valuable insights into the emotional and psychological aspects of mental health, helping him understand the depth and complexity of the issue.

Armed with this new understanding, Instincts worked tirelessly to create a campaign that was both powerful and authentic. He used his photography skills to capture raw, moving portraits of people battling mental health issues. His marketing expertise helped him craft a narrative that was not only compelling but also deeply respectful of the individuals involved.

When the campaign launched, it was an instant success. People were deeply moved by the powerful images and the authentic narrative. It sparked a conversation around mental health that was long overdue, inspiring people to seek help and support each other.

Instincts and Intuition were overwhelmed by the response. Their collaboration had not only raised awareness about an important cause but had also strengthened their friendship. They realized that their shared birthday was more than a coincidence - it was a symbol of their unique connection and shared mission to impact the world positively.
From that day forward, Instincts and Intuition collaborated on many more projects, using their unique gifts to inspire change and make a difference. Their friendship served as a testament to the power of connection, respect, and shared purpose, reminding everyone that when instinct and intuition align, magic happens.

Instincts' campaign was designed to raise awareness about mental health and the importance of seeking help. His idea was to harness the power of storytelling and visual imagery to destigmatize mental health issues and inspire action.

expertise to launch the campaign across various platforms - social media, print, television, and even billboards. This multi-platform approach ensured maximum visibility and engagement.

"YOUR ART IS PEACEFUL WITH A WARRIOR'S POINT OF VIEW."

Your art is peaceful, with a warrior's point of view," suggests a beautiful juxtaposition of tranquility and strength. Seen in a spiritual sense, it conveys the idea of harmonizing the calmness of the soul with the resilience of the spirit.

Imagine a serene lake nestled within a mountain range. The lake's surface mirrors the sky with an unruffled calm, presenting an image of absolute peace. This is your art, serene and tranquil, a reflection of the inner peace within your soul. It captures the serenity of a monk in deep meditation or a dove floating in the vast expanse of the sky.

Yet beneath the lake's placid surface, the water is teeming with life, a silent testimony to the relentless cycle of nature. Similarly, beneath the calmness of your art, there's a warrior's perspective, a relentless pursuit of truth, a fearless exploration of the self. This is the spirit's resilience, akin to a mountain standing tall against the harshest storms, or like a samurai ready for battle, even in the quietest moments.

The art, therefore, is not just a reflection of peace, but also a testament to the courage and determination that comes with a warrior's standpoint. The warrior in this context is not one who seeks to destroy but one who fights for peace, harmony, and enlightenment, much like a spiritual warrior who battles the inner demons of ignorance and fear.

So, "your art is peaceful, with a warrior's point of view," is a tribute to the art that is born from the delicate balance between the tranquility of a meditative state and the strength of a warrior's spirit. The art that doesn't shy away from the truths of existence but embraces them with grace and courage, like a lotus blooming untouched in a muddy pond.

THE STORY OF UNO, THE ARTFUL WARRIOR.

Once upon a time, in a land untouched by the hands of time, there lived an old artist named Ono. Ono was known far and wide for his unusual art – art, that was as calm and serene as a summer's breeze yet as profound and mighty as the winter's gale.

Ono lived in a quaint house by a serene lake nestled within a ring of majestic mountains. The lake, like a mirror, reflected the tranquil sky, while the mountains stood tall and firm, a symbol of strength and resilience. Ono, with his ancient eyes and gentle hands, sought to capture this perfect balance of peace and power in his art.

His canvases were filled with images of the tranquil lake and the mighty mountains. Viewers often remark how his art would make them feel a sense of peace, like a monk in deep meditation or a dove soaring freely across the sky. But beneath this tranquility, there was always an undercurrent of power and strength. The strength of a samurai sword, silent and sheathed, yet ready for battle, or a mountain standing tall against the harshest of storms.

One day, a young man journeyed from a far-off land to meet the famed artist. Upon reaching Ono's home, he marveled at the peacefulness of the lake and the strength of the mountains. When he entered Ono's home and saw his art, he was struck by the same serenity and strength that he felt in the landscape around him.

"Your art is peaceful, with a warrior's point of view," the young man remarked, his eyes wide with admiration. Ono smiled, his eyes twinkling with wisdom. He nodded and replied, "Art, my young friend, is not just about capturing what we see. It's about expressing what we feel and understand. The world around us is a dance of contrasts - peace and chaos, strength and frailty, light and darkness."

Ono gestured towards the lake and the mountains outside his window. "The lake and the mountains are not separate, but parts of the same landscape, much like peace and strength are not opposites but elements of the same spirit. True peace does not mean absence of conflict, but the ability to stand strong in the face of it."

The young man spent many days with Ono, learning to see the world through his art. He learned to see the strength in tranquility and the peace within strength. He learned to paint not just what was visible to the eyes, but also what was felt by the heart. He learned that to truly understand and create art, one must be calm like a peaceful lake but view the world with the insight and courage of a warrior.

And so, the tale of Ono, the artist with a peaceful heart and a warrior's perspective, spread far and wide, touching and inspiring artists beyond the mountains and the serene lake, teaching them the profound lesson of harmonizing tranquility and strength in their art and in their lives.

THE DAMAGED JEWEL

BY MR. SUCCESS STORY

"The Damage Jewel" symbolizes the inner resilience and inherent worth of melanin women who have endured countless moments of hurt and heartache. It draws upon the metaphor of a diamond to convey that these women, like precious gemstones, retain their value and beauty even in the face of immense pressure and brokenness.

Just as diamonds are formed under intense heat and pressure over thousands of years, melanin women have often experienced life's challenges and societal pressures that have tested their strength. Yet, instead of being diminished or shattered by these experiences, they have emerged as resilient, multifaceted beings.

The damage inflicted upon a diamond does not diminish its intrinsic value. In fact, it is through the process of cutting and polishing that its true radiance is revealed. Similarly, the trials and tribulations faced by melanin women have not diminished their worth or beauty. Rather, these experiences have refined their character, granting them a unique brilliance that shines through their scars.

Melanin women, like damaged jewels, possess an enduring strength that stems from their ability to rise above adversity. They embody the power to transform pain into wisdom, and brokenness into resilience. Their stories, struggles, and triumphs become a testament to their indomitable spirit.

"The Damage Jewel" serves as a reminder that the worth of melanin women cannot be eroded by the challenges they face. It emphasizes the importance of recognizing their inherent value, celebrating their strength, and acknowledging the beauty that arises from their ability to withstand and transcend the scars of their past.

THE ADVENTURE OF DISCIPLINE AND CONSISTENCY

Once upon a time, in a world filled with vibrant colors and endless possibilities, lived two best friends named Discipline and Consistency. They were known throughout the land for their unyielding commitment to their tasks and their unwavering loyalty to each other.

Discipline, with his stern but kind eyes, was always ready to jump into action. He was like a sturdy oak tree, standing tall and unwavering, no matter how strong the wind blew. Consistency, on the other hand, was like a gentle stream, flowing steadily day after day. She was always there, never rushing, but never stopping, making small but sure progress.

One day, they met an old sage named Focus who lived in a house shaped like a giant magnifying glass. Focus was famous for his ability to maintain unwavering attention to anything he put his mind to. He explained to them, "You see, every task, no matter how big or small, needs a spotlight of attention. Just like the sun, which nurtures the seedling's growth, your focus can nurture your ambitions."

Inspired by the words of Focus, Discipline and Consistency decided to embark on a journey to find their true Identity and Purpose. They crossed mountains of Doubt and sailed across the raging rivers of Distraction, their bond stronger with every step they took together.

Along their journey, they met Will, a jolly giant with muscles as hard as iron and a laugh as loud as thunder. He was like a giant boulder, steadfast and nearly unmovable. He told them, "I have the strength to move mountains, but it is useless without your Discipline and Consistency. Together, we can overcome any obstacle."

Their journey took them to an enchanted forest where they met Manifestation, a magical fairy with sparkling wings. She lived in a crystal palace that could change its form according to her thoughts. She giggled, her laughter like the tinkling of bells as she explained, "My palace is a reflection of my thoughts and desires. With your Discipline and Consistency, and the strength of Will, you can manifest anything you desire."

Finally, after many adventures, they arrived at the Castle of Identity and Purpose. Here, they met their true selves reflected in the grand mirrors of the castle. Discipline saw himself as a beacon of strength and resilience, while Consistency saw herself as the thread that holds the fabric of life together. They realized their purpose was to inspire others to be disciplined and consistent, to help them manifest their dreams.

And so, Discipline and Consistency, with their newfound friends Focus, Will, and Manifestation, returned to their home, ready to guide and inspire others. They had learned that with focus, will, discipline, and consistency, one could manifest their true identity and purpose.

And so, the story of Discipline and Consistency serves as a timeless reminder. It teaches us that life is a beautiful journey of self-discovery where the seemingly ordinary qualities we possess can lead us to extraordinary destinations when nurtured with focus, will, and manifestation.

And the land was filled with laughter, joy, and growth, as everyone began to understand the spiritual and life lesson that Discipline and Consistency had learned on their adventure. And they all lived happily, with purpose and determination, ever after.

"IF YOU'RE TIRED OF PEOPLE LISTENING TO YOUR CALLS; INCREASE OF BILLS, FORCED UPGRADES, DROPPED CALLS, SCREEN CRACKING, FREEZE-UPS, BLANKING OUT, MINUTES RUNNING LOW, CONSTENT LOW BATTERY, CONNECT TO THE COSMOS. WE USE TELEPATHY OVER HERE."

In a spiritual sense, if you find yourself exhausted by the constant intrusion of others and the negative effects it has on your life, it can be likened to the experience of being tired of people listening to your calls. This metaphor represents a desire for privacy, autonomy, and freedom from external influences.

The increase of bills signifies the burden of obligations and responsibilities that accumulate over time. It could be financial, emotional, or energetic demands that drain your resources. Forced upgrades symbolize the pressure to conform and adapt to societal expectations, often at the expense of personal preferences and values.

Dropped calls, screen cracking, freeze-ups, and blanking out symbolize the interruptions and disruptions in your life. They represent the moments when you feel disconnected, lost, or unable to communicate effectively with others or even with your own inner self.

The metaphor of minutes running refers to the passing of time slipping away, emphasizing the urgency to reclaim control and make the most of each moment. It reflects a sense of time slipping through your fingers, perhaps due to being preoccupied with external distractions or obligations.

Constant low battery suggests a depletion of energy and vitality. It signifies feeling drained, worn out, or lacking the inner resources necessary to sustain yourself. It can be a metaphor for feeling emotionally or spiritually exhausted.

Finally, the call to "connect to the cosmos" implies a desire to tap into a higher source of wisdom, guidance, and spiritual connection. It represents a longing for a deeper understanding of oneself and the universe. By embracing this metaphorical journey, you seek to transcend the limitations of the mundane world and find solace, inspiration, and renewal in a greater cosmic harmony.

"We use telepathy over here" implies a shift towards intuitive and non-verbal forms of communication. It suggests a longing for authentic, genuine connections that go beyond superficial words and external trappings. It signifies a desire to connect with others on a soul level, where thoughts, emotions, and intentions are shared directly, transcending the limitations of language and technology.

In summary, this spiritual metaphor depicts a yearning for personal autonomy, privacy, and freedom from external influences. It symbolizes the desire to break free from the burdens and distractions of the everyday world, seeking deeper connections and a renewed sense of energy and purpose by connecting with the cosmic realm and embracing intuitive forms of communication.

"PEOPLE ARE SO CAUGHT UP LOOKING OFF INTO SPACE THAT THEY ARE NEVER TRULY PRESENT. "

The saying "looking off into space" is often used metaphorically to describe someone who is not fully engaged with the present moment. This can refer to individuals who are physically present but mentally absent, distracted by their thoughts or daydreams. Alternatively, it can refer to individuals who are preoccupied with their phones, computers, or other electronic devices, which can create a sense of detachment from the immediate environment.

When people are "caught up" in this way, they may miss out on important details or experiences that are occurring in the present moment. They may also struggle to connect with others on a personal level or to engage in meaningful interactions. When we are not fully present, we are less likely to notice the small things that can bring us joy, such as the beauty of nature, the laughter of a loved one, or the taste of a delicious meal.

This is not to say that daydreaming or using electronic devices is inherently bad. However, it is important to recognize when these behaviors are preventing us from fully engaging with the world around us. By making a conscious effort to be more present in our daily lives, we can cultivate a greater sense of mindfulness, appreciation, and connection to the world and the people around us.

"IF YOU'RE HAVING AN UNESY DAY, SMOKE SOME WEED AND LAUGH AT EVERYTHING THAT TICKLES YOUR SOUL. IF YOU DON'T SMOKE GET SOME CONTACT THEN WATCH A COMEDY." "LAUGHTER IS AN ENERGY BOOSTER."

Metaphorically and spiritually, we can understand the statement "If you're having an uneasy day, smoke some weed and laugh at everything that tickles your soul" as an invitation to find a source of joy and upliftment in order to ease one's troubles. It suggests using a particular substance, in this case, marijuana, as a tool to shift one's perspective and enhance the experience of laughter.

In this metaphorical interpretation, smoking weed represents an external aid that helps us alter our state of mind and see the world from a different angle. It can be seen as a metaphor for seeking external experiences or influences that can provide temporary relief from stress or discomfort. This could apply to various aspects of life, not necessarily limited to substance use.

Laughing at everything that tickles your soul signifies finding humor in the small, simple, or even mundane aspects of life. It encourages us to embrace a lighthearted attitude, allowing ourselves to be open to laughter and joy. Laughter is seen as a powerful tool in this context, symbolizing an energy booster that can help us rise above our difficulties and shift our focus towards positive emotions.

For those who don't smoke or prefer not to use substances, the suggestion of getting some contact and watching a comedy offers an alternative path. Seeking "contact" could refer to connecting with others who bring positivity and laughter into our lives, or it could mean engaging in activities that have a similar effect. Watching a comedy represents engaging in an activity that brings genuine laughter and amusement.

In a spiritual context, the underlying message could be about the importance of finding joy and laughter as a means to uplift our spirits. It suggests that laughter has the power to raise our vibrational energy and bring us closer to a state of inner peace and harmony. By embracing laughter, we can release negative emotions, shift our focus, and tap into the innate joy and happiness that resides within us.

Overall, this metaphorical interpretation emphasizes the significance of seeking out sources of joy and laughter to navigate through difficult or uneasy times, recognizing laughter as a potent force that can boost our energy and bring about a positive shift in our spiritual well-being.

THERE ARE 3 TYPES OF PRAYERS:
THE CONSCIOUS PRAYER UNICONSCIOUS PRAYER SUBCONSCIOUS PRAYER

In a spiritual sense, prayers can be broadly classified into conscious, unconscious, and subconscious prayers based on the level of awareness and intentionality of the person offering the prayer.

Conscious prayer refers to a deliberate and intentional act of communicating with a higher power, such as God, the universe, or a deity, with a clear understanding of the purpose and content of the prayer. These prayers are typically offered during religious or spiritual practices, such as meditation, worship, or ritualistic ceremonies.

Unconscious prayer, on the other hand, refers to the spontaneous and unintentional expression of one's thoughts and feelings towards a higher power. These prayers may arise unconsciously during moments of intense emotion, such as fear, grief, or gratitude, and may not be accompanied by a clear understanding of the purpose or content of the prayer.

Subconscious prayer refers to the deep-seated beliefs, desires, and intentions that a person holds in their unconscious mind, which may influence their conscious prayers and spiritual practices. These prayers may arise from the subconscious mind's programming, conditioning, or past experiences, and may not be consciously acknowledged or recognized by the person offering the prayer.

In summary, conscious, unconscious, and subconscious prayers represent different levels of awareness, intentionality, and expression in one's spiritual practice, and each type of prayer may have unique benefits and implications for the individual's spiritual growth and well-being.

"BECOME THE LIGHTHOUSE SO THAT YOUR FUTURE MATE CAN SEE YOU."

Imagine yourself standing on the edge of a vast, mysterious ocean, surrounded by darkness. The waves crash relentlessly against the shore, and the night sky is veiled by thick clouds, obscuring any glimmer of hope. In this vast expanse of uncertainty, you yearn for a companion, a partner to share your journey with. But how can you attract their attention, drawing them towards you amidst the endless abyss?

Now, envision a majestic lighthouse towering above the tumultuous waves, its beam of light cutting through the darkness with unwavering determination. This beacon of guidance stands tall and strong, emanating a radiant glow that stretches far and wide. It serves as a symbol of hope, a symbol of a future filled with love and companionship.

To become the lighthouse means to become the best version of yourself, to cultivate your inner light and let it shine brightly. Just as the lighthouse stands as a prominent figure in the vast ocean, you must become a person of substance, radiating confidence, authenticity, and self-assurance. Nurture your passions, ambitions, and personal growth, allowing them to illuminate your path and inspire others.

As your light shines forth, it creates a magnetic allure, drawing the attention of potential partners who are searching for someone just like you. They are captivated by your inner radiance, your unique blend of qualities that sets you apart from the rest. Your light becomes a guiding force, guiding them towards you, like a ship finding its way home in a treacherous storm.

This metaphor holds true for both women and men, emphasizing that anyone can become the lighthouse of their own destiny. It transcends gender, reminding us that we all possess the power to illuminate our lives and attract meaningful connections. By embodying the essence of a lighthouse, you become a symbol of hope, a beacon that cuts through the darkness, allowing your future mate to see your brilliance and be drawn toward you.

So, aspire to become the lighthouse amidst the vast ocean of life. Cultivate your inner light, let it shine brightly, and trust that it will guide your future partner towards you, creating a beautiful union of two souls united by the radiance they found within each other.

In the realm of romantic relationships, there exists a mysterious and intangible force guiding us towards our destined partners. It is a force that resides deep within us, an innate sense that transcends logic and reasoning. This force is known as intuition or instinct, and it serves as a profound tool for recognizing and embracing the presence of our soulmates.

Imagine yourself standing in a lush, vibrant garden, teeming with countless flowers of all shapes and colors. Each flower represents a potential partner, hidden among the foliage. As you navigate this garden, your intuition acts as a delicate and perceptive sense, attuned to the subtle energies that emanate from these potential matches.

Your intuition is like a finely tuned compass, guiding you toward the person who aligns with your deepest desires, values, and aspirations. It is an inner voice, a whisper from your heart, providing insights and signaling when the right person is near. Just as a compass needle points unerringly toward the true north, your intuition points you toward your true love.

Imagine encountering a particular flower that exudes a fragrance that resonates with your soul. Your intuition recognizes the subtle scent as if it were a familiar melody that stirs your emotions. It tingles within you, resonating with a sense of recognition and connection. This is your intuition affirming that this person possesses the qualities and compatibility you seek.

Yet, intuition is not merely a passive observer; it is an active participant in the dance of love. It nudges you to pay attention to the subtle signs and synchronicities that unfold in your interactions. It prompts you to listen to your gut feelings and to trust the sensations that arise within you when you are in the presence of your potential mate.

Just as a skilled sailor reads the winds and the tides to navigate treacherous waters, your intuition reads the unspoken language of energy and emotions. It deciphers the unspoken words and the hidden truths that lie beneath the surface. It allows you to sense the authenticity and resonance between you and your partner, guiding you towards a deep and fulfilling connection.

However, it is important to note that while intuition is a powerful tool, it should be complemented by conscious awareness and discernment. Intuition does not operate in isolation; it works hand in hand with your rational mind. It is through the integration of both intuition and rationality that you can make informed decisions about your potential mate.

So, trust your intuition, for it is a treasure chest of wisdom and insight. Cultivate a deep connection with your inner voice, listen to its whispers, and be attuned to the sensations that arise within you. Allow your intuition to guide you through the garden of potential partners, leading you to the one who resonates with your heart and soul. In doing so, you embark on a journey of profound love and connection, guided by the truth that only your intuition can reveal.

"DON'T "FOLLOW ME", WE FOLLOW GOD, WE GONE BE A MINUTE."

holds several layers of spiritual meaning.

1. **Independence and Self-Realization**: The speaker is expressing that they are not a guide or a leader to be followed blindly. Instead, they are on their own spiritual journey, following the path of God. This suggests a call for individuals to find their own way and establish a direct relationship with the divine, rather than depend on human intermediaries.

2. **Divine Guidance**: By stating "I follow God," the speaker is expressing that their faith and trust in God guides their actions, decisions, and paths in life. This highlights the importance of surrender and trust in divine wisdom.

3. **The Journey**: The phrase "we gone be a minute" connotes that the spiritual journey is not a quick or easy path. It requires patience, time, and perseverance. It's not an instant transformation but a continuous process of growth and learning.

4. **Community**: Although the speaker initially appears to discourage followers, the phrase "we gone be a minute" could also be seen as an invitation. It's as if they're saying, "If you choose to join me in following God, know that it's a long journey, and we'll be in it together for a while." Despite the individual nature of spiritual journeys, it's a subtle signal of community and shared purpose.

5. **Humility**: The quote also reflects humility. The speaker does not set themselves up as an authority or guru, but simply another soul following the path of God. In religious and spiritual contexts, humility is often regarded as a virtue and a recognition that our knowledge and understanding are limited in comparison to the divine.

Therefore, this quote can be seen as a call to embark on one's spiritual journey with patience, humility, and a direct connection with the divine.

www.ingramcontent.com/pod-product-compliance
Lightning Source LLC
Chambersburg PA
CBHW060055100426
42742CB00014B/2838